Get a Pet!

Written by Joe Elliot

Illustrated by Neil Sutherland, Blue-Zoo and Tony Trimmer

p-**e**-**n**, pen!
The pen is sad.

Go and get
a pet!

n-e-t, net!

Is it a pet?

No, a net is
not a pet!

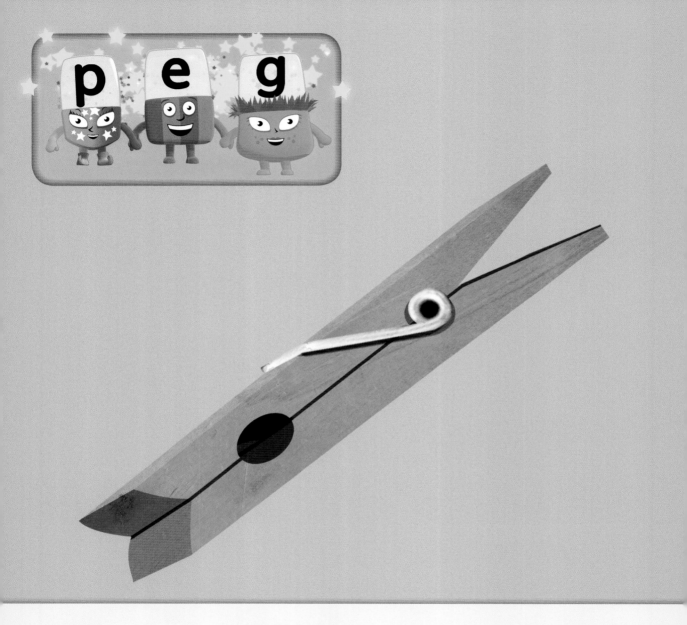

p-e-g, peg!

No, not a peg!
A pet!

p-**u**-**p**, pup!
A pup is a pet!